WALKS ALONG OFFA'S DYKE

Also in this series:

Also: In Spur Venture Guides for walkers and ramblers—

and in Spur County Guides:

Walks Along Offa's Dyke

COMPILED BY

ERNEST & KATHERINE KAY

on behalf of
The Offa's Dyke Association

SPURBOOKS LIMITED

Published by
SPURBOOKS LIMITED
6 Parade Court
Bourne End
Buckinghamshire

At the time of publication all routes used in these walks were correct, but it should be borne in mind that diversion orders may be made from time to time. Maps are not necessarily to scale.

ISBN 0 904978 24 9

Printed by Maund & Irvine Ltd., Tring, Herts.

Contents

Introduction

Offa's Dyke is a great frontier earthwork built in the reign of Offa, King of Mercia, in the late eighth century to mark the boundary between his kingdom in Central England and the Welsh. It is still visible over some eighty miles of its length—in places upstanding to 20 feet from the bottom of the ditch to the top of the bank.

The name was used for a Long Distance Footpath officially opened in July 1971, which incorporated some sixty miles of the best of the remaining earthworks. The Path runs for 168 miles from Chepstow to Prestatyn, mostly through the varied and little frequented landscapes of the Welsh Marches and taking in the Black Mountains and the Clwydian Hills.

This book of circular walks, based on the Path, is compiled from material supplied by Members of the Offa's Dyke Association. This was set up in 1969 to co-ordinate pressure for the opening of the Path. This achieved, the Association has continued in order to bring together the many interests of walkers, historians and conservationists, and those who live and work locally, involved in looking after the Dyke and its Footpath. Its headquarters are at Knighton, Powys (the halfway point of the route) from which address details of membership, publications, accommodation, etc. may be obtained.

This book is divided among ten areas in each of which at least one longer and one shorter route are described. These may be variations on one basic route or entirely separate. They are but a sample of the walks that could be included; major centres such as Chepstow, Kington, Clun, Montgomery and Prestatyn have not been used at all. These routes are no substitute for walking the Long Distance Path itself but for many this is not possible and we hope we are at least giving the flavour of this unique Path and countryside.

Brief linking notes covering the Path between the sections used on the circular walks have been included in the text. Walkers on the round routes will have the advantage of seeing much more than the Path itself.

We are most grateful to Jack Baker, Robin Cain, David Cole, Don Gregory, Frank Noble and Arthur Roberts, who have joined with us in providing the material. We have not tried to impose a unity of style on our correspondents, merely to aim at a consistent level of information.

KATHERINE AND ERNEST KAY

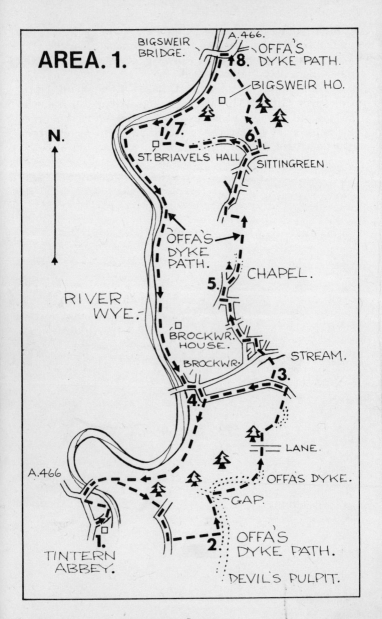

AREA. 1.

BIGSWEIR
BRIDGE.

A.466.

8. OFFA'S
DYKE PATH.

BIGSWEIR HO.

N.

7.

6.

St. BRIAVELS HALL

SITTINGREEN.

OFFA'S
DYKE
PATH.

CHAPEL.

5.

RIVER
WYE.

BROCKWR.
HOUSE.

BROCKWR.

STREAM.

3.

4.

LANE.

A.466

OFFA'S DYKE.

GAP.

1.

2. OFFA'S
DYKE PATH.

TINTERN
ABBEY.

DEVIL'S PULPIT.

AREA 1

Tintern Abbey & Woods, Brockweir

(A) 10, (B) 7, (C) 5½ and (D) 3½ miles.

O.S. 1:50,000. 162; O.S. 1:25,000. SO 50.
Grid references are to these maps.

How to get there: By car: Tintern and Brockweir are on A466 Chepstow-Monmouth road. Tintern Abbey has a car park, some parking is possible at Brockweir, *none* at Bigsweir.

By public transport: Chepstow is the railhead, Red & White Chepstow-Monmouth bus serves all above points.

Refreshments: Tintern has full facilities; Brockweir a shop and public house; nothing at Bigsweir or elsewhere.

Offa's Dyke Path begins in the south at Sedbury Cliffs overlooking the Severn near Beachley and the new bridge. After 1 mile the east bank of the Wye is reached and this is followed leaving Chepstow (with its castle and other historic features; also transport and accommodation) just to the west. The route continues on the east of the Wye but the river is now some hundreds of feet below the well-marked Dyke and Path. The North-South routes of river and of Path and links between them are the subjects of the first walks, starting some seven miles from Sedbury.

These walks use a pair of circuits, a short one Tintern—Path—Brockweir—river and back, 3½ miles (route D) and a longer one of Brockweir—Path—Bigsweir—river—Brockweir, 7 miles (route B) which can be joined into one 10 miles round (A). The longer circuit has a cut-off that can reduce it to 5½ miles (C); this Brockweir—Bigsweir stretch is unusual in having an 'official' alternative Path route. Our round uses both so you are following Offa's Path for the whole route!

Tintern Abbey

Starting at Tintern don't omit a visit to the ruins of the great

Cistercian Abbey, (1) on map (533000). Owned now by the Department of the Environment it is open daily. The Abbey was founded in 1131 but most of what is visible is late 13th century. The remains of the church are most impressive, perhaps the East and West windows in particular.

Tintern itself is a small-scale tourist mecca but the route to Offa's Dyke soon leaves it. From car park at Tintern Abbey, leave by footpath near river passing to right of Anchor Public House and follow through to main road at Police Station. Turn right, go along road a short distance and turn right past disused watermill along formation of disused Tintern Wireworks tramway, crossing river by metal bridge. In a short distance turn left up track with a small area of stone paving at its junction with the tramway.

Rise up to junction of tracks beside stone retaining wall on left: fork right up wide track, shortly fork right (sign to Devil's Pulpit painted on tree) and next left, following above and parallel to lane below, then curving away and climbing up to join forestry road. Turn right, then immediately left at junction of forestry roads where stone directs to the 'Devil's Pulpit'. In 150 yards fork left up smaller track which leads uphill to join the clearly defined and waymarked Offa's Dyke Path at the top of the hill, (2) (542000).

(The Devil's Pulpit itself may be reached by ignoring the above left fork and continuing along the Forestry road until it curves right and downwards under a bluff. Up the bank to the left before the bluff is an ill-defined path leading up a gully to the Offa's Dyke Path 30 yards north of the Devil's Pulpit. This is a limestone crag just under the Dyke with fine views of the valley. 400 yards north along the Path brings you to point (2)).

Turn left to follow the Dyke north to where a modern gap has been cut through a prominent stretch of the earthwork. Pass through the gap and bear left to follow the Path with the Dyke on your left. After 200 yards cross a marshy gap and continue on the Dyke itself. Cross a farm lane, a short stretch further downhill, right and in a few yards arrow signs point your way steeply left through the woods and downhill away from the ridge. Follow the Dyke as a broad bank till where it is ploughed out and then bear right downhill to a gate in the corner of the field. Left through this to reach a vertical post, (3)

(546013), indicating alternative Offa's Dyke routes—left and also bearing right through gate.

First the left route to Brockweir and back to Tintern: a broad track leads in half a mile to Townsend Farm and right into Brockweir village (4) (540011). Left at the farm through gate and follow lane forward for a mile. Where the lane is then paved with stone for a small area turn right to join the track of the disused Tintern Wireworks railway, in which the remains of wooden sleepers can be seen at intervals. Follow this over a metal bridge over the Wye to join the A466 by a disused watermill. Left on road to just beyond the Police station, left down a path signposted 'River Wye 0.2 km.' Shortly fork left past chapel and follow path into Tintern Abbey Car park, (1), to complete route D.

Forward and right through the gate at (3) (546013), the Path leads by small lanes and footpaths with intermittent Dyke to St. Briavel's Common and Bigsweir. This is an area of small farms and houses, well populated but with no villages. First downhill with Dyke on left to cross a small stream and up to the Brockweir-Hewelsfield road. Take lane almost opposite and follow it as it turns left over a stream; left at minor road and immediately sharp right—all this in a couple of hundred yards. The rather muddy lane you are now on emerges on to a road; left, soon swing right and take right fork, (5) (540023), past an old chapel. This road soon peters out and an enclosed path takes you steeply uphill. Left at top and through the farmyard of 'The Fields' (please keep to marked route and close gates) to road. 200 yards right along this and where road bends right take the lane straight ahead; this emerges on another road at Sittingreen, (6) (539038).

Offa's Dyke Path takes the right turn but alternatively the left turn may be taken and the gradually deteriorating road followed steeply downhill. At the bottom keep St. Briavels Hall on your left and pass between stone pillars to the river bank, (7) (531040). Turn left towards Brockweir and 1½ miles has been cut from the route (Route C).

The main route from Sittingreen does not keep to the road for long: take a narrow path left in a hundred yards. Right at a T junction of paths and in a few yards left to slope very steeply downhill through woods for ¼ mile. Continue in the same direction across a field and diagonally left down towards a stone bridge visible in the corner of the next field. Right along drive (left goes to 18th century Bigsweir House) to A466 at Bigsweir Bridge, (8) (540051).

Walk 25 yards towards the bridge and left across stile by the end of the bridge. Something under 3 miles of easy riverside walk will bring you to Brockweir at Quayside just east of the bridge. This stretch has excellent views across the river and up to the woods and there are no path problems. (After under 1 mile the short cut from Sittingreen to St. Briavels Hall described above is met). In Brockweir turn up the pleasant village street. First right, (4) (540011), leads to the way to Tintern described above which completes the full 10 miles circuit (route A).

(The 7 mile circuit (B) starts at Brockweir Street. First right, (4) (540011), to Townsend Farm and left to broad track to main Dyke Path at (3) (546013). Then left to Bigsweir and back to Brockweir as described).

So far the Path has followed good stretches of the historic Dyke on the escarpment high above the Eastern bank of the Wye. This continues North for nearly 4 miles beyond Bigsweir, almost to Highbury Farm. There, quite abruptly, the Dyke disappears and the Path drops down to the Wye at Redbrook. There is now a major gap in the continuous Dyke as far as Bridge Sollers, west of Hereford, and the Path does not pick it up again until north of Kington over 50 miles away. The next routes are set in the Wye Valley going North from Redbrook into Monmouth.

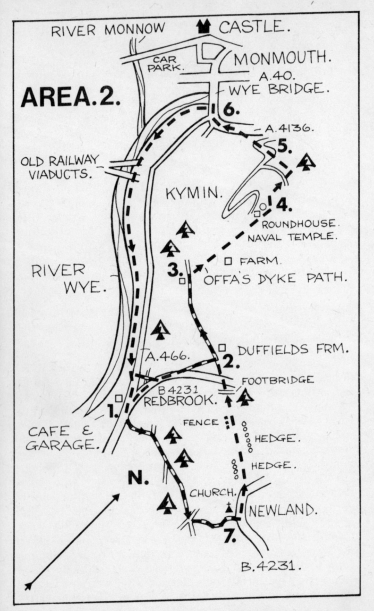

RIVER MONNOW   CASTLE.

CAR PARK.

MONMOUTH.

AREA. 2.

A.40.

WYE BRIDGE.

6.

A.4136.

5.

OLD RAILWAY VIADUCTS.

KYMIN.

4.

ROUNDHOUSE.

NAVAL TEMPLE.

RIVER WYE.

FARM.

3.

OFFA'S DYKE PATH.

A.466.

DUFFIELDS FRM.

2.

FOOTBRIDGE

B 4231

REDBROOK.

1.

CAFE & GARAGE.

N.

FENCE

HEDGE.

HEDGE.

CHURCH.

NEWLAND.

7.

B.4231.

14

AREA 2

**Redbrook, Kymin and Monmouth; with Newland extension
8 and 6 miles.**

O.S. 1:50,000. 162; O.S. 1:25,000. SO 50, 51.
(Former on Newland Extension only)
Grid references are to these maps.

How to get there: By car: Monmouth is on the A40 (T) Ross-Abergavenny road, there is a large car park off Monnow Street near the old Monnow Bridge (505123); A466 connects to Hereford (north) and Chepstow (south). Redbrook is on this last road 3 miles south of Monmouth.

By public transport: Red and White buses connect Monmouth to Newland, Redbrook and Chepstow, also Hereford, Ross, etc.

Refreshments: Monmouth is a major town; Redbrook has pubs, shops and a cafe at the large garage on the west of the road, Newland a pub and shop.

Offa's Dyke Path descends to Redbrook from the heights to the east of the Wye at Highbury Farm. The route then climbs the prominent hill of the Kymin (Naval Temple) on its way to Monmouth, an easy alternative follows the Wye going north from Redbrook. Combining these two makes an easy 6 mile round. An extension takes in the Forest of Dean village of Newland with its 'Cathedral of the Forest'.

From Wye Valley garage and cafe at Redbrook (1) (536102), cross A466 and take service road to left above main road and in front of houses. This passes between village houses and in 300 yards emerges on B4231 just above bridge over the road from an old colliery incline. Right up road and in ¼ mile take track forking left with cottage between road and track. In walking up the valley road you will have passed sundry ruined buildings from Redbrook's past as an industrial village in the Forest of Dean complex: in this case dependent on water power, the remains of furnace ponds are to be seen higher up the valley.

Follow track upwards as at the top of the slope it swings 90° to left, (2) (537108). Pass farm buildings (Duffields) on right and continue to reach barn on left, (3) (530116). Opposite turn right over stile into field and aim uphill halfway between farm on right and trees on left. The path is not evident on the ground and keeping parallel to power line on right is the best guide. Cross stile in far corner of field and continue forward now keeping fence on left. Then through gate into wooded area to reach the National Trust owned area at the top of the Kymin. Cross car park and continue forward keeping the Naval Temple and Round House viewpoint on the left, (4) (528125)—but of course divert to visit them! The buildings were erected by members of a Monmouth dining club about 1800 in honour of the Royal Navy 'to perpetuate the names of those noble Admirals who distinguished themselves by their glorious victories for England in the last and present Wars.' It makes a pleasant place to pause and take in the view to the Black Mountains over the Monnow and Wye Valleys.

With the buildings on the left and still going northwards *avoid* the stile straight ahead but turn sharp left down stone steps. After about 200 yards cross stile on right and keep on downhill with fence now on left. Cross stile by large house and head diagonally right across large field. Cross into wood and swing left continuing downhill to come out on small road, (5) (523129), (this has zigzagged downhill from the top of the Kymin and can provide a bad weather alternative). Straight ahead on road and where this bends sharp right take footpath signposted Monmouth straight on. This emerges on A4136 five minutes walk from Wye Bridge, (6) (513127).

The riverside route back to Redbrook starts here; it is of course the beginning of the walk if done Monmouth—Redbrook—Monmouth. However most walkers will wish to see something of Monmouth and/or seek refreshment. The town has the Shire Hall in Agincourt Square with the Castle remains off Castle Hill just opposite (birthplace of Henry V, hence Agincourt!). St. Mary's Church has a splendid tower but is mostly Victorian; the main street is wide and leads to the unique 13th century fortified gatehouse on the Monnow Bridge.

Returning to the riverside path the route will be seen clearly signposted Redbrook just to the east of Wye Bridge. Immediately keep to the right of a privet hedge by a sports pavilion and keep to the edge of playing fields. The path is clear thereafter by the riverside past former railway viaducts and a (not too obvious) sewage works. After over 1½ miles the A466 becomes a near-neighbour but the path continues in the fields by the river until joining the road quite near Redbrook village. Down the road to the Wye Valley garage and cafe, (1).

The Newland extension to the route starts in Redbrook village. From garage cross main road and turn right. Just past the church take slope and then turning left uphill between school and hall on narrow lane. This soon becomes unsurfaced and climbs steeply. Where it levels out take right turn at T junction with very broad track. In 200 yards take upper (left) fork by electric pump. Across the valley to your right Highbury Farm and the Dyke going south is evident. Climb slowly to junction of several paths. Take left enclosed unsurfaced track leading down (before starting on this, step a few paces to the right for a splendid view to Newland Church).

At the bottom the lane in 100 yards becomes surfaced. First left to pass between church on left and almshouses on right to B4231, (7) (553095). The church ('Cathedral of the Forest') is splendid and large for a tiny village; most of what is seen is 13th to 15th centuries with tombs and brasses. Turn left past the Ostrich, shop and bus stop. In 300 yards, past speed de-restriction sign, turn left at 'Upper Redbrook' footpath signpost.

The paths on this next section are not visibly trodden out but by closely following this route walkers should not go astray. In the first field head diagonally across field to cross gate in angle on left. Forwards with hedge on left (do *not* get into woods on right). Just before top of rise cross gate on left and continue in same direction as before through several fields but with hedge now on right (beware of sticky patch at a spring). Eventually route crosses a stile and continues in the same direction with post and barbed wire fence on left (and splendid view up Kymin on right). Cross lower part of next field with wood below route on right; over stile and down into wood ahead. Cross fence (no obvious stile) into next field to stile and bridge to the B4231 at Upper Redbrook.

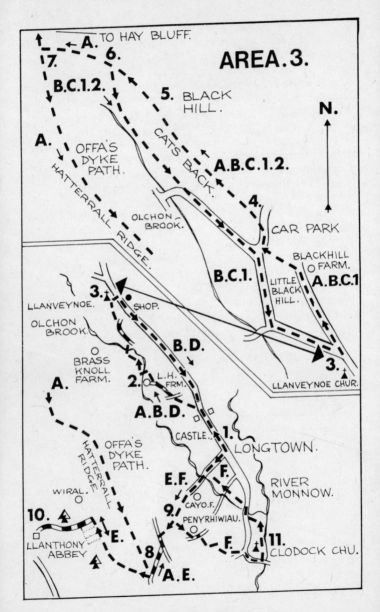

TO HAY BLUFF.

A.

7.

6.

B.C.1.2.

AREA. 3.

5. BLACK HILL.

N.

A.

OFFA'S DYKE PATH.

CATS BACK.

A.B.C.1.2.

HATTERRALL RIDGE.

OLCHON BROOK.

4.

CAR PARK

BLACKHILL O FARM.

B.C.1.

LITTLE BLACK HILL.

A.B.C.1

LLANVEYNOE.

3.

SHOP.

OLCHON BROOK.

O BRASS KNOLL FARM.

B.D.

A.

2. O L.H. FRM.

A.B.D.

3.

LLANVEYNOE CHUR.

CASTLE..

1. LONGTOWN.

OFFA'S DYKE PATH.

HATTERRALL RIDGE.

WIRAL. O

E.F.

F.

RIVER MONNOW.

9. O CAYO.F.

PENYRHIWIAU.

10.

LLANTHONY ABBEY

E.

8.

A.E.

O

F.

11. CLODOCK CHU.

18

AREA 3

Longtown and Black Mountains

**(A) 16, (B) 12½, (C1) 8½, (C2) (or 5½) (D) 4,
(E) 7½ and (F) 3½ miles.**

O.S. 1:50,000. 161; O.S. 1:25,000. SO 22, 23, 32, 33.
Grid references are to these maps.

How to get there: By car: Longtown is on a turning off the A465
Abergavenny-Hereford road; left at Pandy Inn 6 miles from
Abergavenny, then 4 miles via Clodock. (Llanthony is also off
the A465—turn left 1½ miles south of the above at
Llanfihangel Crucorney).

By public transport: Very occasional Yeoman Motors bus
from Hereford to Longtown.

Refreshments: Longtown has inns and village shops;
Llanveynoe a miniscule shop 100 yards from the Church;
Llanthony and Clodock have inns.

The Plain of Monmouth—between that town where Area 2
ended, and the Black Mountains—is not our favourite part of
the Offa's Dyke Path. However, though fairly flat, it does have
attractive villages such as Llantilio Crossenny (which has a
splendid music festival each May) and the finest castle directly
on the route—the mainly 13th century White Castle. With its
moat and towers this is for many people a fantasy castle made
real. Beyond this there are attractive link routes to be found
between the Path and the isolated peak of Skirrid. An
alternative route has been worked out northwards from
Monmouth which misses out White Castle but takes in those at
Pembridge, Skenfrith, Grosmont and Longtown on the way to
the Black Mountains and generally keeps to higher ground.
North of the A465 Abergavenny-Hereford road both routes
climb to the ridges of the Black Mountains: the next walks are
centred on Longtown and take in stretches of each.

Longtown is a remote, straggly village lying under the
shadow of the Hatterall Ridge of the Black Mountains to the

west and with the end of the Cat's Back Ridge to the north. The castle consists of a stone keep (of about 1300) on an earthen motte in a large rectangular enclosure pierced by the modern road; the ruins are currently being consolidated by the Department of the Environment.

The complete round described below (Route A) is a splendid and very full day of 16 miles and only recommended for good walkers in fair weather with clear visibility since much of it is on the ridges of the Black Mountains. A variation cuts off 3½ miles (route B) and makes some of the remainder walking on minor roads. Route B itself splits into alternative circuits—of 8½ (C1) (with a 5½ mile variant (C2)) and 4 miles (D), the last being very simple. As a bonus the Longtown-Hatterall-Llanthony walk is worth doing there and back (E-7½ miles) with a shorter round to Clodock (F-3½ miles). Longtown itself is on the 'Castles alternative' to the official Offa's Dyke route which runs north-south on the Hatterall and is used extensively on route A.

From Longtown Castle—routes (A), (B) and (D)—(1) (321293), walk north along the road for ¹/₃ mile. Beyond Perthi-Pertion, where there are cottages on both sides of the road, cross stone stile on left and head 45° right away from the road to pass through lower of two iron gates. Keep hedge on right, cross stile to surfaced lane, straight down this for 20 yards and then straight on through iron gate by corrugated iron shack. Bear left downhill on drive to Lower House Farm.

Circle round farm keeping buildings on left to reach stile crossing to path just above farmhouse, and down to cross footbridge over Olchon Brook, (2) (309303). Turn right with hollow way to left and stream to right. At waterfall bear slightly left to cross stone stile. Keep hedge on left through field and bear right away from Brass Knoll Farm in next field, then down to footbridge.

Cross corner of field heading upwards to cross stile (corrugated iron) and aim gradually uphill to stile to reach cart track. Where cart track bends right, cross old stile straight ahead in corner of field. Cross field towards Llanveynoe Church.

Leave field by gate in corner and out to road by track, (3) (304314). Turning right on this road the village shop and post office is reached in 100 yards and continuing takes one back to Longtown to complete route (D). Route (C1) *starts* on the road by Llanveynoe Church, were a car may be left, and picks up the route of walks (A) and (B), the start of which has been described above.

Coming out of the church, (3) (304314), turn left and after 150 yards take right fork at New House. This lane ends by Blackhill Farm; through gate straight ahead and after 20 yards through old gate on left. Bear right following fence on the right through old holly trees and take left of 2 iron gates. Continue uphill with old hedge on left to just below top of Little Black Hill. Through gate, turn right and reach metalled lane. Turn right along this (left returns to Llanveynoe and Longtown). In 150 yards car park and picnic site are reached (4). (288327). (The 8½ mile circuit (C1) can be reduced to 5½ (C2) while keeping the best of the view by starting the walk from here). Sign on left of car park says 'Black Hill, Offa's Dyke Path 4.8 km.' Cross stile as indicated by this and head upwards for the top of the ridge—the Cat's Back. Where ridge broadens take the right hand side.

Eventually the trig. point on top of Black Hill, (5) (275348), is reached. Bear slightly left keeping on top of the ridge with drop to your right for about ½ mile. The infant River Olchon may then be discerned in a distinct depression ahead and to the left of the track. Before reaching this, if walking routes (B/C), (for route (A) see below), turn sharp left, (6) (266353), along a narrow track to reach the stream just above a ruined building. Do not take the path crossing the river at this point but continue downhill. Shortly, the Olchon Valley suddenly comes to view, and the path continues downwards, with the river to the right, in places quite steeply, for a further mile before joining the road. To the right will now be seen a picturesque grouping of ford and bridge: the route continues straight on down the road, a narrow, little-frequented lane with for some distance fine views to the right across the Olchon Valley. After a mile a lane to the left diverges to reach the picnic place and car park to complete route (C2): but if you continue along the little road for a further three miles you pass through Llanveynoe (completing route (C1)) to reach Longtown (end of route (B)).

Route (A) continues forward from (6) (266353) and swings

21

slightly left with steep drop on right. The trig point on Hay Bluff (Pen-y-Beacon) is soon visible in the distance ahead to the north-west; head for this. A mile short of it and a mile beyond the path leading to the Olchon Valley meet the Offa's Dyke Path, (7) (253360), descending on the left from the end of the Hatterall Ridge, at a crossing of paths. There are no signposts. Turn left (note prominent rock outcrop on right) to climb 100 feet steeply south-east to the brow of the ridge; it is worth carrying a compass.

Once on the ridge the path is well trodden with occasional waymarking and there is then a 7 (yes, seven!) mile stretch south-eastwards along the ridge with good views in all directions. After this distance a distinct dip in the ridge with a crossing of paths is reached, (8) (308270). Longtown appears behind and to the left whilst on the right paths lead down to Llanthony, visible in the valley of the Honddu. Take the path leading steeply diagonally downhill on the left, which can be followed to Longtown as in the return leg of walk (E) below.

Route (E). If you fancy a 7½ mile walk with Llanthony Abbey as its destination and involving a stiff climb across the Hatterall in both directions, start south down the road from Longtown Castle. Then, just beyond the Northants County Education Authority's Field Centre, turn right down a road marked with a T sign. Follow this across the river Olchon, through to Cayo Farm and pass to the right of the farm buildings. The route then runs uphill through fields with the hedge on the right. In the second field the route to Clodock (route F) bears to the left, (9) (313283), on a marked track.

For Llanthony, carry on up to a prominent line of trees crossing the path. Go through the gap in the line of trees at the right hand edge of the field, diagonally across the next field, and through iron hurdles into a short lane, with trees on each side, on the right. At the end of the lane go through a wooden gate, up a bank, and you come to a well defined cross track. Turn left, and after about 200 yards, just before the scanty ruins of a building, take the track on the right slanting uphill between trees. Follow this diagonally up the mountain to reach the ridge, (8) (308270). You have now climbed 1,150 feet from the River Olchon.

On the other side of the hill the track to Llanthony can be

seen going diagonally down the mountain on the right, passing above a wood. Presently you come to three small fields on the left of the path: turn left after these down a track which leads through a narrow wood to the considerable ruins of Llanthony Abbey (10) (288277). The ruins of this largely Norman Transitional priory of Augustinian Canons are extensive. The Half Moon Inn is 200 yards right up the main road for less spiritual refreshment.

Returning to Longtown by the same route is very pleasant, giving quite a different set of views. On top of the Hatterall Ridge (point (8)) route (A), see above, joins you for the descent to Longtown. An alternative way to this point from Llanthony is to ascend to the first of the three fields referred to, then turn left to Wiral (instead of right). Just before the farm take track sharp right uphill. Where this peters out continue in the same direction to reach the summit ridge by a trig point. Right and in ½ mile point (8) is reached.

Route (F) is a short round walk Longtown–Clodock. It is not all well marked but is quite practicable provided care is taken. Start the same way as route (E) as far as point (9), two fields beyond Cayo Farm.

Follow the track diagonally across the field, left handed coming from Longtown, go into the next field, passing above small disused quarry and over stile, then just to right of a pond with larch trees around it, left where track from right is joined, to pass through iron gate into farmyard (Penyrhiwiau), then immediately right through another gate, past bungalow on left, then left down a sunken road.

At the first gate on the right where road drops, enter the field ahead, and leave it through a gap in the opposite hedge, diagonally to the right. In the next field there is a stone slab forming a rudimentary stile in the bottom right hand corner. Cross this, turn left, and keep hedge on left for the next two fields. When you come to three iron gates, go through the central one and cross the next field diagonally, aiming to the right of Clodock Church which is plainly visible. Go through iron gate, in 20 yards over stile on left, across a small dingle, diagonally across corner of field over stile and onto the road. Many of the stiles on this route are formed by a large flat slab of stone bedded on its edge.

Turn left along the road to the church, (11) (327275), which is worth a visit for its unusually complete early 18th century furnishings and fittings in a Norman setting.

Continue along the Walterstone Road and turn left just before the bridge over the River Monnow. The path runs between churchyard and river, along the river bank, then through orchards to reach the road again at the bridge over the River Olchon. Turn right across the bridge, then immediately left to follow the path near the river, passing across a lane, to the right of the sewage works, and turn right where it joins the outward route at the next lane. Turn left at the main road in 300 yards to bring you back to Longtown Castle.

(Longtown—Llanthony—Clodock—Longtown joining routes (E) and (F) is a 9 mile alternative).

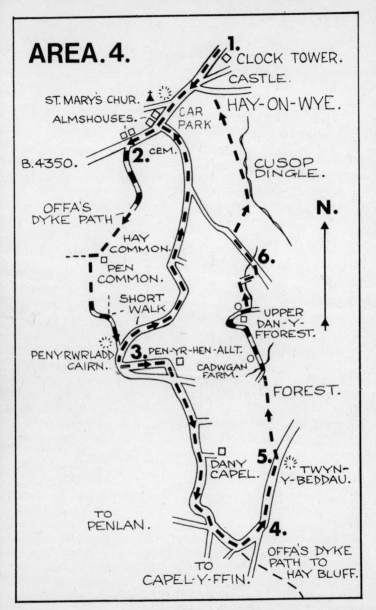

AREA. 4.

1. CLOCK TOWER.
CASTLE.

HAY-ON-WYE.

ST. MARY'S CHUR.
ALMSHOUSES.

CAR PARK

B.4350.

2. CEM.

CUSOP DINGLE.

OFFA'S DYKE PATH

N.

HAY COMMON.

PEN COMMON.

SHORT WALK

6.

UPPER DAN-Y-FFOREST.

PENYRWRLADD CAIRN.

3. PEN-YR-HEN-ALLT.

CADWGAN FARM.

FOREST.

5.

DANY CAPEL.

TWYN-Y-BEDDAU.

TO PENLAN.

4.

TO CAPEL-Y-FFIN.

OFFA'S DYKE PATH TO HAY BLUFF.

26

AREA 4

South of Hay-on-Wye
9 miles or 4½ miles

O.S. 1:50,000. 161 (**not** 148); O.S. 1:25,000. SO 23 & 24.
Grid reference are to these maps.

How to get there: By car: Hay can be reached from Hereford via the A438; from Cardiff via Merthyr and Brecon; from the North via Leominster. There are adequate car parks, the largest behind the castle off Oxford Road (229423).

By public transport: Hereford is the railhead. Buses—Midland Red and Red and White—are not frequent. There is also a service from Brecon.

Refreshments: Hay is well served with accommodation and a full range of refreshment places. Nothing else on the routes.

The last chapter had us walking in the Black Mountains above Longtown. According to which of two alternatives is used, the Path reaches the Northern summit ridge either just East of or at top of Pen-y-Beacon (Hay Bluff). From here there is a magnificent view northward over the upper Wye Valley (the same Wye as at Chepstow!) and into the South Radnor uplands. Underneath you is the Hay-Capel y ffin mountain road and then the farmed slopes leading down to Hay-on-Wye. The next walks are in this area between the Mountains and Hay and are best approached from the latter.

The Town:

There is no evidence of a settlement at Hay until the closing years of the 11th century. The name 'Hay' derives ultimately from the Norman-French word 'la haie', a hedge. When Bernard de Newmarch, a Norman Baron, began his conquest of the old Welsh kingdom of Brycheiniog (from which the modern name Brecon originates), he appears to have granted the land round Hay to one of his followers, another Norman named William Revell. Revell established a simple castle and a

27

church on the site of modern Hay in the early years of the 12th century.

Within a few decades the original castle was replaced with a larger stone-built one a few hundred yards to the east—a structure which still survives, although in a fragmentary state. At the foot of this second castle a walled town was built, enclosing about 60 acres and reaching right down to the banks of the Wye—"one of the most compact military strongholds on the Welsh Border."

There is no doubt that Hay's main reason for existence in the earliest days **was** military: to secure and hold recently conquered territory and to control movement along the Wye Valley. As such, the town and castle were frequently fought over, captured, burnt: by King John in 1216; by Llewelyn the Great in 1231; possibly by Owain Glyndwr in the last bid for Welsh independence in 1402.

Today there is little left of the original castle and the town walls and gates have disappeared completely. With the ending of the Welsh wars, Hay became a quiet market town. Today it is best known as the centre for the 'world's largest' second-hand bookshop (in the castle, the old cinema and several other buildings).

The Walks:

There are two walks described here, both of them circular walks starting and finishing in Hay, the shorter covers about 4½ miles; the longer covers nearly 9. Both show to good advantage what Hay and the foothills of the Black Mountains have to offer in the way of unspoilt scenery and intriguing history. Since both walks start off the same, they will be described together.

Start from Hay Clock Tower (1) on map (229425) in the centre of Hay and set off up the main street (Belmont Road, the B4350 to Glasbury, Brecon and West). At the top of the hill you will pass on your right a small cafe which occupies the site (or near enough) of the old West Gate of the walled town of Hay. And a little beyond, and also on your right, is a castle mound, probably the site of William de Revell's first castle. Just beyond is St. Mary's Church. Founded in 1120, it is as old as the town itself. Carry on along the B4350 past two groups of early 19th

28

century almshouses built in the 1830's 'for the reception of . . . poor, indigent women'. On the left hand side of the main road opposite the second terrace of almshouses is the entrance to the town cemetery, a lychgate set back from the road, (2) (226419). Just to the right is a track curving away out of sight skirting the edge of the cemetery. A sign on the gable wall of a house tells you that this is the Offa's Dyke footpath. You turn left off the main road here and join the track. After a slow start the track begins to climb. The cemetery is on your left behind a high hedge. The banks on either side of the track get higher and higher as you carry on; the gorge of the small stream trickling alongside the track begins to take on impressive dimensions; the trees on either side of you grow together over your head.

After about half a mile the track comes to a gate. Go through and you are in an open place; this is the edge of Hay Common. Carry on following the track as it angles across to the left slightly and then turns sharply uphill. Keep the big hedge just on your right hand. In the distance the small building you see is Pen Common Cottage. The Common itself is on your left. The humps and bumps in the ground are all that remains of a once thriving community, for this is a classic example of a deserted Medieval village—settlements like it are known throughout Britain. It used to be thought that the Black Death in the 14th century was responsible for desertions of villages. And although the role of the plague must not be discounted, we know now that rapacious landlords, war and changing agricultural practice played a part in the years between 1100 and 1500.

Carry on up to Pen Common Cottage, turn right, and after 50 yards turn left and carry on uphill, keeping the hedge on your left. Pass through two gates and the path turns once again into a track. As you top the rise to this second gate, you find the Black Mountains looming large before you. They contrast markedly to the gentle Wye Valley and the Hills of Elfael at your back.

The Black Mountains derive their name from their curious colour and not, as some have suggested, through any reference to the Black Arts, those most Welsh of Welsh things: magic and witchcraft. Still, many spine-tingling local legends about the Black Mountains have filtered down to modern times. Perhaps

the most quietly sinister are the tales concerning the Old Lady
of the Black Mountains, who lured travellers to their deaths in
mists and at night. Those who had no alternative but to cross
the mountains were advised to place a bowl of water at the foot
of the maypole at nearby Craswall to ward off the attentions of
the Old Lady.

Mindful that you have taken no such precautions, press on
carefully down the lane. In a few hundred yards you join
another track. Turn right and keep right through another gate.
Soon you should come to the remains of Penyrwrladd
chambered cairn. Originally a cairn 60 feet long and half as
wide, it concealed two burial chambers, both of them made of
slabs of stone. The monument dates from the Neolithic (the
New Stone Age) and was in use some 4,000 years ago. A few
yards beyond the cairn you join a metalled lane, (3) (226397).

If you are taking the shorter walk, turn left down the lane and
follow it down into Hay. The walking is easy and you are
unlikely to meet any traffic beyond the occasional tractor.

If you are taking the longer walk, turn right at the lane and
follow it uphill for about a mile and a half, passing Dan y Capel
farm and a right-hand turning for Penlan and on until it joins
the lane from Hay to Capel y ffin. (4) (241379) Here you turn
left and follow the lane downhill. This is as near as you will get
to the Black Mountains on this walk though the route up to
Hay Bluff, altitude 2,219 feet, the promontory nearest you, is
obvious. The next one, looking west, is Darren Lwyd (The
Tumpa) which is 2,263 feet high. Between the two is Gospel
Pass, through which the lane you are standing on passes on its
way to Llanthony Priory and the enchanted Vale of Ewyas.

But you are going the other way, down the lane. The Mound
you pass is Twyn y Beddau, Welsh for 'The Hillock of the
Graves'. It is almost certainly a Bronze Age tumulus dating
from the second millenium B.C. Local tradition, however,
claims the mound and the area round it as the site of a
particularly bloody battle fought in 1093 between Rhys ap
Teudwr, the last independent ruler of South Wales, and an
English Army. Rhys was killed along with thousands of his
followers and the nearby Dulas Brook is said to have run red
with blood for three days.

Just beyond Twyn y Beddau, (5) (242387), fork left off the

lane, and, keeping the large forest of conifers just on your right, carry on downhill through a gateway and into a narrow lane. You ford a stream before passing Cadwgan Farm (a lovely old farmhouse) where the lane becomes surfaced as it picks its way down a very steep slope and on to another farm at Upper Dan y Fforest. At the farm the path turns left off the lane (it is not marked) and carries on downhill, hugging the left bank of a small stream. Eventually you will come to a footbridge and after crossing it, the way angles off to the right across a meadow and joins another surfaced road, (6) (237408). Turn left and follow the road for about 300 yards, past a fine holly hedge, coming finally to a gate on the right hand side of the lane. Go through into the meadow and angle across it to the left where you will pick up the last stretch of the path as it moves down Cusop Dingle on the left bank of Dulas Brook. The Dingle is thickly wooded but it is possible to make out the houses of Cusop village through the trees. You are in Wales here, looking across into England. The path is clear and leads through kissing gates and past doleful ponies, right to Hay. Up a narrow alley between buildings—you emerge, blinking, by the car park at the foot of Hay Castle.

On its way North from Hay the Path leaves the Wye to climb attractive valleys and hills to the hamlet of Newchurch and then the village of Gladestry. Over Hergest Ridge and then into the market town of Kington beyond which we pick up the Dyke again for one of the very best stretches of the route.

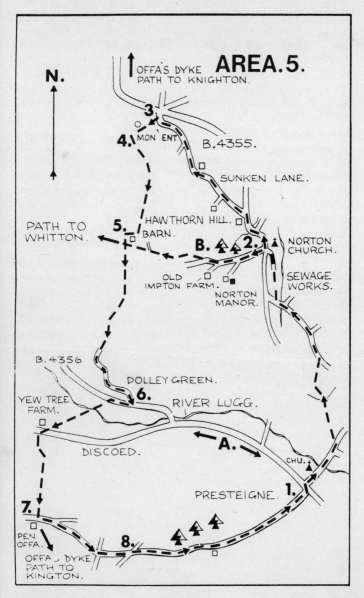

N.

OFFA'S DYKE PATH TO KNIGHTON.

AREA. 5.

3.

4. MON' ENT

B. 4355.

SUNKEN LANE.

HAWTHORN HILL. BARN.

PATH TO WHITTON.

5.

B. NORTON CHURCH.

2.

OLD IMPTON FARM.

SEWAGE WORKS.

NORTON MANOR.

B. 4356

DOLLEY GREEN.

6.

RIVER LUGG.

YEW TREE FARM.

DISCOED.

A.

CHU.

PRESTEIGNE.

1.

7.

PEN OFFA.

8.

OFFA'S DYKE PATH TO KINGTON.

32

AREA 5

Presteigne

10 miles, with two possible short cuts reducing it to 6½ miles.

O.S. 1:50,000. 148; O.S. 1:25,000. SO 26, 36.
Grid references are to these maps.

How to get there: By car: B4360, 4362 from Leominster, B4355 from Knighton.

By public transport: Staples bus from Leominster (infrequent).

Refreshments: Presteigne has full facilities, shop at Norton.

The walks so far have looked at two areas in the lower Wye Valley and two in the Black Mountains. We now move north to the 14 splendid miles of Path in Radnorshire, mostly on or by the fine Dyke, from Kington to Knighton. Many attractive circular walks can be found in this stretch: here is described one long one (with short cuts) linking Presteigne with the route.

Presteigne, on the Lugg, is the old Radnorshire shire town. Somehow it is more 'English' than most border towns with its handsome Georgian houses and Norman/Decorated church.

Leave Presteigne town centre. (1) (314644) via Broad Street, pass church, cross river; road is now called Ford Street. Pass Stapleton Hall in under ¼ mile on right; just after this cross the stile on the left (beyond old shed). Diagonally cross two fields: second field on slightly raised path. Turn left across stream. Diagonally cross field and cross stile on right end of old copse (under electricity cables). Turn left into lane for under ¾ mile.

Cross stream by bridge and immediately on right cross stile, keeping stream on right, go through gap in hedge. Go through gate to left of Sewage Works and another gate ahead (at far end of Works). Keep in same direction (hedge on left), passing farm on right. At end of field cross stile (house on left) and continue forward on road, (stream below on right). Road turns left and joins B4355.

Turn right (north) along main road past Norton Church, (2)

(304673) on right (shop is on the left). Continue for ¼ mile on Main road which turns right and climbs to just past derelict cottage on left and turn through gate into metalled track on left and contour, through another gate (where footpath joins on left). Keep on metalled track until it bears left, then take sunken lane ahead.

At crossing track, take gate into left field ahead, following sunken lane on right. Cross two fields and one gate before rejoining track via gate into it. Follow track towards farm ahead, eventually passing in front of farm on right. Turn right by side of farmhouse on to metalled road which climbs and eventually joins B4355, (3) (287688). (Hill House entrance is opposite). Turn left through gate **just** before joining road onto track between two hillocks (Monument ahead). Below Monument, to Sir Richard Green Price (1803–87) who brought railways to Radnorshire, bear left to stile on Offa's Dyke Path, (4) (285687). Do not cross this stile, but turn left (south) on line of Dyke.

Cross next stile to west side of Dyke. Path continues on Dyke, which is a well marked feature, up Hawthorn Hill and comes down gradually on west (right) side of hill past a corrugated iron barn, (5) (283674) on well signposted track. Continue with wire fence on right until just above plantation, where path strikes across field past signpost and downhill, cross a stile, go through two iron gates, the second leading into a green lane between overgrown hedges. Continue down enclosed track to B4356 at Dolley Green, (6) (284655).

Turn right on road and in about 100 yards take track on left into field. Continue on left side of field to footbridge, and on left side of next two fields to cross road at Yew Tree Farm. The Dyke here becomes a massive feature with a deep ditch on the west. The path continues on the top of the Dyke uphill to lane at Pen Offa Bungalow, (7) (269639). (Just beyond the road, an original gap through the Dyke can be seen).

Leaving Offa's Dyke Path at Bungalow turn left along road to green lane about 100 yards on right through gate. After a time left hand hedge peters out but lane continues along right hand hedge to gate at green lane cross roads. Continue straight ahead between wire fence and hedge to junction with metalled road, (8) (283634). Turning left along road continue on it to

Presteigne (about 2 miles) avoiding all side roads etc. and passing County Primary School on left on outskirts of town. By Green near housing estate take left fork to Clock Tower and Town Centre, (1) (314644).

Two **short cuts** save 2 and 1½ miles respectively on this route.

First (A) by turning left down the B4356 at Dolley Green, (6), Presteigne may be pleasantly reached in just over 2 miles.

For the second (B) leave Norton by minor road on left opposite church at point (2) and follow lane forward through gates for nearly a mile until Old Impton Farm. Fork right through gate beyond pond leaving farm on left and in 30 yards take ill defined track on right across field between two large trees to reach iron gate. Go through gate and follow well marked track, keeping left at end of small conifer plantation, through gates, climbing steeply with sharp drop to left. Cross field at top of hill, ignoring well marked track bearing to right in field, to join Offa's Dyke footpath on left of corrugated iron barn near sign post, (5) (283674).

The northmost stretch of the above route (by the Green-Price monument) is little over two miles from Knighton, which may be reached by the Path following good Dyke all the way.

AREA 6

Knighton, Offa's Dyke Park, etc.
8 miles and 3 miles.

O.S. 1:50,000. 148 or 137; O.S. 1:25,000. SO 27 and 37.
Grid references are to these maps.

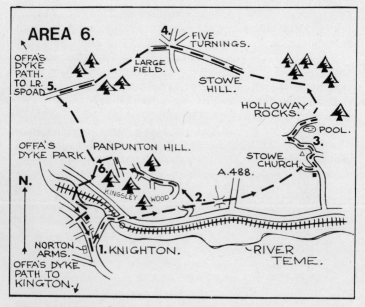

How to get there: By car: A488 from Shrewsbury and north;
A4113 from Hereford and Ludlow. Large car park behind
Norton Arms in town centre (286723).

By public transport: 5 trains daily (except Sundays) on
Central Wales line—Shrewsbury to Swansea. Bus service,
several a day (Teme Valley) from Ludlow and, more
irregularly, (Owens Motors), Newtown and Presteigne.

Refreshments: Knighton has ample facilities, accommodation,
etc.

Knighton (Tref-y-Clawdd, i.e. the 'town on the Dyke' in Welsh) is the halfway point on both Path and Dyke. A compact and unassuming little market town, it has a special place in our affections as the setting for the official opening of the Long Distance Path in 1971 by Lord Hunt and as the centre for most Offa's Dyke activities, including the Association. The castle flourished in the 12th and 13th centuries (now a large mound at the top of the town) and the church tower is medieval. Offa's Dyke Park, the work of the local Tref-y-Clawdd Society, is off West Street and includes a fine stretch of Dyke. The old Primary School by the Park is being converted for use as a Youth Hostel and is also an Offa's Dyke Information Centre.

The town, set in the deep valley of the Teme, is a good walking centre. Here is one very pleasant route, with a short alternative, set to the north of the town; the ODA have published several others.

From Norton Arms, (1) (286723) take Station Road opposite past Knighton Station. Turn right on Clun road (A488). After 50 yards take green track on left which continues just above the road through lower part of Kinsley Wood. Where path meets horseshoe bend of metalled track, take lower arm.

At next bend, (2) (298728), go straight ahead over stile and across field towards big hedge in field beyond, crossing a footbridge. Take stile to road (A488) and iron gate opposite, proceeding with hedge on left. Go through series of gates; after first field, hedge is on right. (Views back to Kinsley Wood).

At top of ridge go through wooden gate and descend by hollow way directly opposite to broad unsurfaced farm track— right on this till it meets surfaced road—turn left up to Stowe Church, (3) (311737) (St. Michael) (Pevsner in 'Buildings of England' refers particularly to the beautiful setting, and says the masonry is medieval, the dressings renewed. He mentions also the good wooden roof, and an 'Arts and Crafts' reredos of 1901).

Continue on track circling to north-west behind church. At head of cwm near old quarry, go through wooden gate on right and take principal track forking right. Continue up valley (views back to Knighton and Radnor Forest). Bend right above pool on left, and continue upwards on track. Go through iron gate, circle left and then right, keeping in valley bottom as it climbs through Holloway 'Rocks'.

Emerge onto the green turf of Stowe Hill with new woodland a short distance to right. Turn slightly left over crest of hill due north (no visible track). Just over summit, reach wire fence by woodland, turn left along it and continue with fence on right through gates. (At end of woodland, fine views to right to Caer Caradoc hillfort in near distance and Stretton Hills beyond). After about 1 mile on ridge, track becomes enclosed lane— continue on this to main road (A488) at Five Turnings, (4) (286754).

Cross main road to grass track through iron gate opposite (**not** gate marked New House Farm). A short distance up track cross gate and muddy area into large field. Cross field diagonally (no clear path) to junction of two belts of woodland at top corner. Continue in south-easterly direction on green track with hedge on left, trees on right. Cross iron gate. 200 yards beyond, Offa's Dyke and the Long Distance footpath crosses track at belt of trees, (5) (276749). Turn left over stile with 'acorn sign'. (Views to Knucklas Viaduct and Castle to west are excellent).

It is two miles from here into Knighton and no difficulties should be found in following the route. The Dyke, though never very pronounced, is your constant companion and the Path is well used and quite clear—but you will have a lot of stiles to climb. You will soon reach Panpunton Hill which is the highest point visible from Knighton and where a Countryside Commission flag (white acorn on black background) was flown on the day the Path was opened. Knighton is clearly visible from here.

The route now starts to descend and just before reaching the end of Kinsley Wood, (6) (285735), it turns sharp right and steeply downhill. At the bottom of the hill cross the Knighton-Llanfair Waterdine road and the railway and the bridge specially rebuilt over the Teme. Follow the riverside path and then up the steps into the Offa's Dyke Park by the stone commemorating the Opening. Through the Park to West Street by the Information Centre, left and your starting point is reached.

A pleasant short walk (A on map) may be had by cutting from point (2), (298728) to point (6), (285735) across the top of Kinsley Wood. It can be extended by walking on the Dyke from the latter point to the top of Panpunton Hill.

Just before the path would rejoin A488 Clun road it joins a loosely metalled surface with two horseshoe bends: the main route described above goes forward down at the first horseshoe and over the stile straight ahead. The Kinsley alternative goes forward up at the first horseshoe.

Climb with this and just beyond the first bend in 200 yards take a very steep track striking up on the left into the woods. Near the top of the slope, right at T junction with a broader track. Keep to this track as it crosses a summit, falls and starts to rise again gently. Avoid a prominent left turn but just beyond this take a left small green path at fork. Right at T junction and forward to gate (sign on **other** side says 'Beware Adders' but don't worry you are coming from the other side!).

Left down side of field to cross fence by Offa's Dyke Path signpost and so back down the left side of the field towards Knighton.

Between Knighton and Lower Spoad west of Clun (Norman castle and ancient bridge) is some of the wildest and best of both Path and Dyke including the latter's highest point (1,408 feet). Springhill just north of this is the standard spot for visiting parties to see a 'good continuous stretch of Dyke'.

AREA 7

**West of Bishop's Castle, and Kerry Hill Ridgeway
(A) 9, (B) 5½ and (C) 5 miles.**

O.S. 1:50,000. 137; O.S. 1:25,000. SO 28.
Grid references are to these maps.

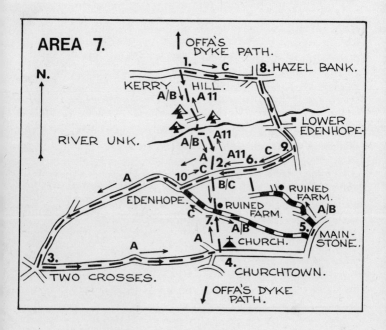

How to get there: These three walks start 4½ miles west of
Bishop's Castle (22 miles from Shrewsbury on A488; Ludlow is
18 and Craven Arms 10 miles away). Detailed intructions to
reach the starting point are given below. Valley Motors run a
Shrewsbury–Bishop's Castle bus service but there is nothing
nearer the route.

Refreshments: Town facilities at Bishop's Castle; apart from
this bring your own as you will not find anything on the walks.

The high Dyke continues north of Clun until beyond the Kerry Hill ridgeway north of which it drops down to the plain of Montgomery and the Severn Valley. The Clun-Kerry Hill stretch is one of the most tiring to walk—the usual appellation of "switchback" explaining why. Sparsely populated, little visited, it remains one of the most exciting parts of the Path and the following walks are in a small way testing as well as most enjoyable. They start at a height of 1,300 feet and never drop below 900 and are over wild hilly remote country with wide views. Underfoot it is often wet and muddy so suitable footwear is a necessity.

Bishop's Castle, with its 1,000 years of history, is an attractive and busy little market town (a borough until 1967). Its hilly main street has the Parish church with Norman tower. at one end and the 18th century Town Hall at the other and in between most of the architectural styles of the past 200 years.

To get to the starting point go down the main street of Bishop's Castle and turn right at the Parish Church. Continue on this narrowing road for about 3 miles until Bishopsmoat is reached, noting on the right a well-preserved Norman motte. At the crossroads take the middle road labelled PANTGLAS, go past a telephone kiosk at Hazel Bank and park your car on the grass verge, (1) (258896), where the Offa's Dyke Path crosses the Kerry Hill Ridgeway.

WALK A

Climb over the stile to the South, as the Offa's Dyke fingerpost bids you and clamber on to the path, which soon skirts a forest of conifers to your right, before entering it at a waymarked stile. The track now slopes quickly into Nut Wood, at the bottom of which lies the little River Unk, a tributary of the River Clun, which it joins at the town of that name, later to be swallowed up in the Teme. Cross the Unk by the plank bridge and make for the path on the Dyke, which can be seen climbing up the steep bank opposite. Once up the hill, the path soon levels out to reach the narrow road that runs at right angles to it along Edenhope Hill, (2) (263883). This is a good moment to stand and stare. As you draw breath, take in the spectacular scenery of the Clun Forest with Corndon Hill away

41

to the North-East, and if you are birdwatchers, look out for buzzards soaring above Edenhope Hill.

Suitably refreshed turn right, leaving Offa's Dyke for awhile, and enjoy the luxury of walking along the level grass-bordered road, which runs east–west. You are still over 1,300 feet above sea-level here and, although you will soon lose a little height as the road crosses a cattle-grid and becomes unfenced, you will still have the feeling of being on top of the world as you come to Two Crosses, (3) (240868). At the crossroads take the left fork down a narrow road, which will soon drop into a well-wooded valley with splendid views of the tree-covered hillside opposite you to the south. This lonely, little-used road leads down to Churchtown, (4) (264874), to use the rather grand name given by the O.S. to a hamlet of several houses, a white caravan and a church. Here the Offa's Dyke Path comes down from the north to the valley floor before quickly climbing again to the south. The earliest settlers here were probably traders making a living out of supplying the needs of those who used the Dyke. The church is the parish church of Mainstone, a village a mile away to the east. Just before you reach the church, which is on your left-hand side, turn left on to the Offa's Dyke Path again, as it climbs sharply to the North. After about half a mile a wide grassy track crosses the path from the north-west. Turn right on to this track, once again taking your leave of Offa's Dyke. After walking to the South-East for a few hundred yards you will find that the track enters a field through an open gate. Keep close to the hedge, which will remain on your left-hand side and the track, which at times becomes a sunken lane under overarching trees, will take you to the village of Mainstone, (5) (275876).

Mainstone is an isolated spot, named after a large boulder, which according to local tradition was used as a test of a man's strength. Turn left and walk on the metalled road for a hundred yards, then turn left again at the chapel. Follow the winding grassy track up to a barn on the skyline. The adjoining farm, now completely in ruins, once boasted the name of King Gwilliam. The track divides here. Take the path to the left and keep on it for about a quarter of a mile until it reaches a gate at the top of the hill. Climb over the gate and at once turn right on to a small path which skirts the hedge. Follow this field-path which, after passing a pond, leads to a gate on to the Edenhope Hill Road, (6) (267884). Turn left onto this road and you will soon see the Offa's Dyke stile on your right (2) which you will have crossed earlier. Back over the stile then, and retrace your steps down to the Unk valley. Pass over the plank and go back through Nut Wood. Before long you will see your car on the Kerry Hill Ridgeway (1) (258896).

WALK B

(This is a shortened version of Walk A, devised especially for those who, after reaching the country road that runs along Edenhope Hill (2) (263883), feel that they may have bitten off more than they can chew).

Cross the road and move South once again on the Path, which at this point runs along the Dyke and soon winds its way by easy stages over the top of Edenhope Hill. It is as well, along this stretch, to beware a number of rabbit holes in the Dyke. Before long you will come to a scene of desolation; on your left is a ruined farm, with the slate roof lying more or less intact on the ground, and on your right is a grove of gaunt, dead trees. Here the hill begins to fall away and you will soon find a grassy lane running transversely across your path, (7) (263878). Turn to the left here and leave Offa's Dyke, as you follow the grassy lane down to Mainstone. (For the details of the rest of this walk, look back at the directions given in Walk A).

WALK C

From the same starting point turn round and walk down the lane in an easterly direction, past the telephone kiosk to the crossroads, where you take the road to the right at Hazel Bank, (8) (269896). This road soon becomes a steep and narrow lane winding down to the Unk valley. Shortly after crossing the little river the road divides, the left-hand fork leading to the nearby Lower Edenhope Farm. Take the road half-right, which climbs sharply for about a quarter of a mile. At (9) (275887) the road takes a 90° turn to the right; if you were to go straight on, you would soon find yourself in a cul-de-sac, leading to a farm. Turn right then, and you will be on the Edenhope Hill Road, whose wide grassy borders offer the walker a pleasant alternative to the high hard road.

The gradient is easy, the views magnificent; Clun Forest opens up ahead, as the highest part of the road is reached. Soon a stile on the right indicates the place where the Offa's Dyke Path crosses the road, (2) (263883). Almost opposite, the Dyke rises to the South. Take to this path on the left, which here coincides with the Dyke and which almost immediately climbs up towards the nearby summit of Edenhope Hill. Beware the rabbit holes, which abound on this section of the path. Just before the path begins a sharp descent, you will pass a ruined farm on your left and the skeletons of dead trees on your right. A minute later, the path meets a wide grassy track, which crosses the path in a north-west south-easterly direction, (7) (263878). Leave the Dyke here, and turn right towards the north-west. Continue on this track for rather less than half a mile, where the track joins the Edenhope Hill Road at (10) (258882). Turn right again and walk along the hill road for about 300 yards until the Offa's Dyke stile comes into view on the left at (2) (263883).

The rest of the walk is on the long-distance path. Cross the stile and moving northwards drop down into the Unk valley. Before you lose much height, look up to the hilly country in the north-east, where, if you are lucky, you will be rewarded with a view of Corndon Hill on the skyline. The Dyke disappears for a while into the valley, but you will soon see the little river Unk, which you will cross by a plank. A way-marked stile points the way to a steep and slippery path through Nut Wood. Once up this well-wooded hill the path leaves the trees and rejoins the Dyke in open country. Together path and Dyke soon return the walker to the Kerry Hill Ridgeway.

The next stretches of Path going north are generally pleasant but unexciting. We pass east of and close to Montgomery (and later Welshpool), from both of which circular walks can easily be worked out. Then over Beacon Ring Hill Fort on Long Mountain to cross the Severn at Buttington and up the towpath of the old Montgomery Canal and the Severn itself, with the Breidden Hills prominent to your right. We regain high ground north of Llanymynech where old Roman mineral workings are to be found and continue north towards Oswestry (Area 8).

44

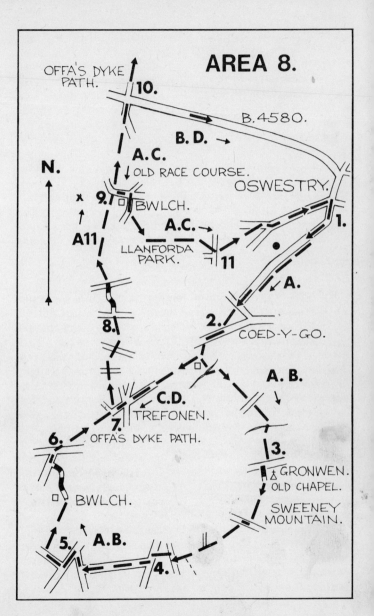

AREA 8.

OFFA'S DYKE PATH.

10.

B.4580.

B.D. →

A.C.
OLD RACE COURSE.

OSWESTRY.

N.

x

9. □ BWLCH.

A11

A.C. →

LLANFORDA PARK.

11

1.

•

A. ↓

2.

COED-Y-GO.

8.

A.B. ↓

C.D.

TREFONEN.

7.

OFFA'S DYKE PATH.

6.

3.

GRONWEN.
OLD CHAPEL.

SWEENEY MOUNTAIN.

□ BWLCH.

5. A.B.

4.

AREA 8

Oswestry, Sweeney Mountain and Trefonen
(A) over 11, (B) under 10, (C) 7½ or (D) 6 miles.

O.S. 1:50,000. 126; O.S. 1:25,000. SJ 22
(mostly) and SJ 23.
Grid references are to these maps.

How to get there: By car: A483 Chester-Swansea trunk road; 2 miles off A5 London-Holyhead.

By rail to Gobowen on Chester-Shrewsbury line. Trains about every 2 hours, then frequent Crosville bus (2 miles).

Refreshments: Two pubs at Trefonen, no others on the walk. Plenty of choice in Oswestry.

The Dyke has been intermittent for most of the stretch since Kerry Hill (Area 7) but is very evident again in the few miles to the old Oswestry racecourse which are included in this chapter.

Oswestry has a long history, ranging from a bloody battle between Penda of Mercia and Oswald of Northumbria in the 7th century to the expansion as Cambrian Railway headquarters in the 19th. At some unknown even earlier time was the construction of Wat's Dyke east of the town, whose course is interrupted by the conspicuous Iron Age earthwork of Old Oswestry. The railway has gone but the Norman castle mound, the Dyke and earthwork remain. In the 18th century it was pointed out that the eclipses of the sun in Aries had been fatal to the town, for there were disastrous fires in 1542 and 1567, in both of which years the sun was eclipsed in that planet! But there have been many other fires since King John burnt the town in 1215.

To traverse any of Offa's Dyke from Oswestry one must follow a triangular route, and Trefonen is a good place at which to join the long-distance path. For a flying start, take the morning or early afternoon bus (Crosville) from Oswestry (different times on market days, no service on Sundays); otherwise start the walk by the Welshpool road, turning into

Penylan Lane at (1) (288292) just beyond the Brook Street signals.

Penylan Lane is narrow but not busy, and for nearly half its length one can walk behind the hedge, along the edge of the playing fields, where rather surprisingly there is a public footpath. The lane ends at a T-junction; cross the stile ahead and at the end of the long field take the stile, not the gate, and so at the next stile reach the road at Coed y Go, (2) (273277), and turn right.

After 100 yards, opposite the end of a block of former cottages with large upstairs windows (built for weavers, perhaps?) a path from a tall stile crosses a field to a group of farm buildings (Gwern). (To their right a stile marks the well-trodden path across the fields to Trefonen—2½ miles from the start—routes (C/D)).

For the longer walks go through an iron gate left of the buildings: the path skirts a boggy patch to a stile under a holly, then bears right to a stone slab bridge before resuming its south-westerly direction, shown by stiles, to cross a road. In the second field beyond the road, strike across to the bottom right-hand corner; beyond the gate, turn right across the brook and climb the bank keeping a tall holly hedge on the left. At the far end of this hedge the path crosses a stile, then continues by the right-hand hedge in three fields to Gronwen, (3) (278264).

Just beyond the double bend a footpath sign points along a drive to a former chapel. From this, make for the gate to the *right* of the farm; in the far corner of the next field a stile leads to an embanked track—not a forgotten fragment of Wat's Dyke but a former quarry tramway, though where it ended on the north is not clear. It now makes a pleasant introduction to Sweeney Mountain, a modest height surmounted by a folly (not accessible) and crossed by several paths.

When the embanked track reaches a road (one can visualise the former level crossing) turn right for a few yards to a field gate on the left, from which a path leads by a right-hand hedge. In the second field, where a wide view opens up to the left, do not follow the track leading up to a larch plantation and a farm, but continue over the field at the middle level to its far end, where in the right-hand corner will be seen an iron gate fastened with a nut and bolt, with a rustic 'stile' alongside, from which a green track runs forward leaving a deserted stone house on its right. The track becomes better defined as it climbs through pleasant woodland (ignore a left downhill fork) until it reaches a gate and stone stile. The use of a thick stone slab placed vertically as the main part of a stile is common in these parts, but this one is unusual in having a hole through it to act as a step.

Bear right along the lane for some hundred yards, then left from a stile with steps by a visible path across one field to a road. Nearly opposite, a flight of steps shows the start of a continuing path, but at the time of writing this is obstructed further on, so it is safer to follow the 'Treflach' sign from the road junction below, (4) (267249).

At the far end go right from the triangle junction. Below to the left, within the curve of the road, is a short well-preserved section of Offa's Dyke; it may be reached by a corner-cutting path from a stile and steps opposite the white gate of a bungalow, but to continue the walk it is just as quick to follow the road round the corner as far as the first building, opposite which a green track will be seen sloping up to the right, (5) (258249). In the second field the original track may have kept at the same upper level (and it still leads to a good area for blackberries) but as there is a steep-sided quarry ahead it is better to drop through the bracken to another terrace track (another tramway?) leading to the far bottom corner of the open hillside, and so along a green lane to a road opposite old quarry cottages.

Before the road drops to a working quarry entrance bear right up a rough track, and when this curves to the left continue ahead by a really green lane which leads to a farm called Bwlch (though nothing so impressive as a bwlch is to be seen) and then becomes a made road. At its end turn right and at the next junction, (6) (250262), look for the Dyke Path sign, from which the way is clear across fields to Trefonen (6½ miles from Oswestry by this route). From the village centre the "No Through Road" past the school gives a direct return to Oswestry, but just before the road drops to the centre an Offa's Dyke Path sign, not very conspicuous on a yellow brick wall, points the way northward, (7) (259267). There are two pubs and a shop in the village, where the north-south road runs along the line of the Dyke.

The long-distance path, after crossing two roads, regains the Dyke as it reappears after a ploughed-out section, and shortly climbs to run along the top of a particularly massive stretch. At the lane junction, (8) (256279) the Dyke can be seen descending ahead but the path alongside it has been lost and one has to follow the road through a smelly haulage yard to the site of Llanforda Mill, where the painted acorns are usefully accompanied by arrows to show the line of path.

On the climb through the wood the path is on a substantial causeway, a reminder that in the past the hill-dwellers returned from the mill with loads on their backs or on those of their animals. However, they would not have turned up the steep slope as the Path does: look carefully for acorn signs here and if one seems to be missing from a junction go back to the last one, as there are numerous misleading tracks in the wood. Before long the path is at the top of the wood following the Dyke itself, of which the commanding position becomes evident when just beyond a stone chair (convenient resting-place) the view opens out at a five-ways, (9) (255298). From this point the Dyke Path continues north (not straight ahead, but through the gate and then sharp left) and soon reaches the Old Racecourse, a large area of common 1100 feet up on which to wander and enjoy the extensive views over Wales. The Dyke is now out of sight, down to the left.

For an easy return to Oswestry turn right down the B4580, (10) (258310). The alternative requires some careful route-finding but is more varied and interesting, and it is rather longer if one has followed the Dyke Path as far as the Old Racecourse.

For this route, return to the five-ways at (9) (255298) and turn uphill by a broad track through a small bwlch to a farm of the same name. Turn right past the buildings and just beyond the pond go half-left through a fieldgate to the furthest corner of a large field and cross the right-hand ditch and hedge. There may be no stile here, but beyond it a stile can be seen to the left leading into a spinney; there is another stile on the far side of the spinney, the way to which may be somewhat overgrown, but after emerging into the fields the rest of the route is easy.

49

Keep forward through two field-gates, then when the ground starts to fall steeply bear right to the gate at the bottom corner of the field. Beyond is the park of Llanforda Hall, a pleasant area with some fine trees: the Hall is no more, but the wall of the walled garden can be seen. The way lies not far to the right of this, through two gates, the second leading into a wood; at a junction take the right-hand track which leads out again into the park. The path here is not obvious but the general direction is half-left, roughly along the line of the power poles until a drive can be seen below. This leads to a road by a new Public Footpath sign competing with a "No Admittance" board on the gate. Opposite (11) (274288), the drive continues for half a mile after which the way is clear by roads to Oswestry.

The full round (A) is over 11 miles; returning to Oswestry down the B4580 from point (10) saves 1½ miles (B). A further 4 miles may be cut by going direct to Trefonen (point (7)) from point (2), (routes (C/D)). Other permutations can be worked out by the walker.

The Path follows excellent stretches of Dyke north from Oswestry and past Chirk Castle—early 14th century but lived in continuously and open to visitors. After crossing Telford's A5 we reach the Llangollen Canal and turn along its towpath leaving the Dyke heading for the industrial area of Acrefair. Apart from a few traces near the north coast this is the last we see of the Dyke as the best of the rest of it is to be found amidst the industry of Wrexham and Rhos; the Path takes a more westerly course along the Clwydian Hills. The towpath soon crosses the magnificent Pontcysyllte Acqueduct over the Dee and most walkers will pass that way although the official route uses the Dee Bridge in the valley below—so the area covered in our next walks is reached.

AREA 9

Llangollen, Valle Crucis, Eglwyseg and Dinas Bran
9 miles or 7 miles with optional extras.

O.S. 1:50,000. 117; O.S. 1:25,000. SJ 24.
Grid references are to these maps.

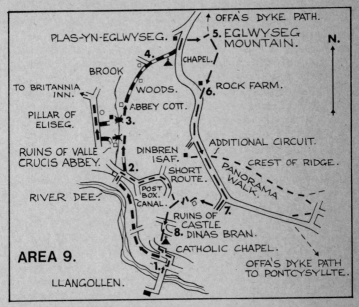

AREA 9.

How to get there: By car: A542 to Valle Crucis (205442), car park serves both walks; A5 to Llangollen, car park between A5 and A539 approached from Market Street (214420) for longer route.

By public transport: Rail to Ruabon and Crosville bus to Llangollen. Bryn Melyn Motors, Llangollen operate local services.

Refreshments: Full range in Llangollen. Nothing elsewhere on route; Britannia Inn is 1 mile from Valle Crucis.

The Path passes north-east of Llangollen to climb to the Panorama or Precipice Walk (a small road in fact) and proceed northwards. Our next walks link this stretch of the Path with the International Eisteddfod town of Llangollen and sites which tell the story of the Princes of Northern Powys, who held this frontier against Offa and then Norman invaders.

The route starts at the northern end of the bridge over the turbulent Dee, (1) on map (215422), the only noteable ancient feature in Llangollen. Fifty yards east of the bridge a road to Minera, World's End and Eglwyseg turns sharply uphill and swings left below the Llangollen feeder of Telford's Shropshire Union Canal. Leave the road before crossing the hump-back bridge and follow the towpath north-westwards to where the A542 crosses it. Continuing along the towpath to the next bridge over the canal, and turning back up the A542 for a hundred yards provides a pleasant way to the gate on the bend which is marked as the access to the local Rifle Range, (2) (208435). A field track from this gate leads to a path which continues to the bank of the Eglwyseg brook opposite *Valle Crucis Abbey,* and turns down to cross a footbridge just beyond the ruins. The path continues along the side of a field of caravans, providing rather incongruous neighbours for the finest monastic ruin in North Wales, then turns left to the car-park and entrance.

The Abbey is maintained as an Ancient Monument, open throughout the year. Among the architectural details in the Abbey it is worth noting the finely carved tombstone of Madog ap Griffith. He was the grandson of the Madog who founded this Cistercian Abbey in 1201, and was himself the last Welsh prince who was able to rule Northern Powys effectively from Dinas Bran. Much of the castle masonry there seems to date from his period.

Continuing up the track which provides access to the car-park and turning right on the main road, the **Pillar of Eliseg** can be seen on a green mound on the right-hand side, two fields along. It is the remains of a 9th century memorial cross from which the valley, and the Abbey, took their names of 'the Vale of the Cross'. The faint inscription honoured Eliseg, Offa's contemporary and traced the ancestry of the ancient kings of Powys back to Vortigern and to his wife's father, Magnus

Maximus, the commander of the legions in Britain, who was killed in 383 A.D. trying to make himself Emperor of Rome.

From the pillar you retrace your steps a hundred yards to the little lane down to a farm building, and down across the field to another footbridge over the Eglwyseg brook, (3) (205444). From this the path climbs to the left, crosses a ladder stile and follows the hedge northwards. The route turns right along the drive which runs from Abbey Cottage to the track running through the woods on the lower slopes of Fron Fawr and turns left to continue northwards along it.

This pleasant track continues for almost a mile, passing a farm and a few scattered houses before it joins the very minor metalled road from the A452, (4) (208458), and continues eastwards along it for another half a mile to the Eglwyseg chapel-of-ease at its junction with the road from Llangollen to World's End.

It is possible to save almost a mile of harder walking by turning right up this road to where the Offa's Dyke Path joins it above Rock Farm, (6) (218453), but to get a better impression of this stretch of the long-distance route, where it runs along the scree below the dramatic white crags of the scarp of Eglwyseg Mountain, turn left down the road to the farm buildings in the bottom of the valley.

There is a remarkable difference between the landscapes produced by the older Silurian rocks around Llangollen and these Carboniferous limestone crags to the north and east of them. The Silurian mudstones, flags and shales form steep but rounded hills, with few outcrops of bare rock, providing rough grazings for cattle and sheep, among spreads of gorse and bracken, where the sheer limestone crags are capped by sandstones and grits forming bleak, open, heather and bilberry-covered grouse moors.

Opposite the last farm building at Plas-yn-Eglwyseg, a right-of-way through a farm gate leads up into a hollow, crosses it into a field on the left to follow the hedge below the wood and join the Offa's Dyke Path at the ruins of Pen-yr-erw, (5) (220463). The limestone scree, below the sheer scarp, is embedded in red clay and carries more varieties of plants, with yew and mountain ash trees, dog violets, rock-rose and yellow wort among the flowers. Jackdaws and kestrels nest in crevices in the cliffs above.

From Pen-yr-erw we turn right. In the other direction the Offa's Dyke Path climbs steadily northwards along Llwybr-y-Fuwych, the old drovers' track to the market of Wrexham. Turning south into the hollow and slanting up into the scree covered slope beyond, our route reaches the thousand-foot contour, four hundred feet above the Eglwyseg brook, before it descends to other derelict buildings in the next hollow and continues along a broad track to join the Eglwyseg road above Rock (or Tan-y-graig) Farm, (6).

The route follows this road for half a mile before the road turns down to Llangollen at a point where another metalled track continues on through a gate. This is the start of the 'Panorama Walk' laid out in Llangollen's expansive 19th century era as a resort, when George Borrow made it his headquarters for his exploration of 'Wild Wales'. Our route follows another mile and a half of the Panorama Walk before turning off to climb the isolated hill of Dinas Bran, which appears to the right after we top the second gentle rise.

(**A detour over the tops.** The steady trickle of cars in summer may add to the restlessness of those walkers who would prefer to be up on the top of the limestone scarp. Just before the ground begins to fall away more steeply on the right, a path through Dinbren Isaf farm comes out at a gate on that side (221 441) and opposite it a track slants up to the left and climbs one of the deep gullies in the face of the scarp. The path then follows an old wall up to the right to a track along the far side of the battered Eglwyseg plantation. This track swings left and then right onto the crest of the ridge (at 236 438) above the 1,300 foot contour. From here the track commands views out over the towns and villages of the North Wales coalfield to the Cheshire plain, as it leads down to the road which runs along the edge of the open moor. A path cuts to the right across the corner between the track and this road, and just beyond the junction with the lane coming up from Acrefair, another path along the slope to the right provides a short-cut over to the Panorama Walk at the point where the Offa's Dyke Path, coming up from the south, joins it. From here it is a mile and a half back along the Panorama Walk to the Dinas Bran approach, and the whole circuit adds more than three miles and a stiff five hundred foot climb to the walk).

The route to **Dinas Bran** leaves the Panorama Walk along another metalled lane coming steeply up from Llangollen on the neck of the spur, (7) (227433), but leaves it after a short distance over a stile to the right, from which it aims across the hollow for the path which can be seen ascending the steep slope of the spur towards the ruins. When this ascent eases it is best to keep to the right, along the crest of the steep slope for the easiest crossing of the deep defensive ditch which also seems to have been the quarry for most of the stone from which the castle was built. This way leads through the narrow gatehouse entrance to the level grassy platform of the courtyard, around which stand the battered remains of the great hall, towers and curtainwalls of the 13th century castle. The site had been occupied by the fortifications of earlier princes of Powys, and the name of Dinas Bran and the fainter earthworks surrounding it suggest that it may have been occupied in the Dark Ages, and perhaps in even earlier periods when security was more important than comfort or ease of access.

From Dinas Bran the line of Offa's Dyke Path can be traced beyond where it descends at Trevor to link up briefly with the Llangollen Canal, on its approach to where Telford's great cast-iron aqueduct, on its pillars 120 feet high, can be seen striding across the Dee valley. Beyond that the Path comes to Offa's Dyke itself, pushed back here onto the edge of the plain, out of sight of the princes of Powys.

The path from the other end of the castle, overlooking Llangollen, descends even more steeply on a zig-zag course, then continues across a slight hollow to swing left along the hedge at the end of the open ground, through a gate into a lane, and down across another lane, (8) (217428). Where the lane bends sharply left, continue down through the wicket gate ahead, along the hedge to another gate into a path which runs between the school playing fields and the Catholic Chapel. This leads back to the Eglwyseg road at the canal bridge, completing the circuit, and back to the bridge over the Dee and Langollen's main streets.

A Shorter 7 mile Circuit can be walked by starting from the car park at Valle Crucis, walking the route from there to Dinas

Bran, but returning without descending to Llangollen:

At the foot of the steep descent from Dinas Bran, (at 218 430), look out for a path turning down through the bracken on the right, to a swing-gate into a field. The path runs down alongside the hedge, and along the bottom side of the field to a stile by a field gate onto the Eglwyseg road. Five hundred yards up this, fork left along the lane which leads down to the main road at the Ty-du post-box (209 435). Just along the main road to the right is the gate and the track to the Rifle Range, and to the path back to Valle Crucis by way of the footbridge across the Eglwyseg brook, (3) (205 444).

The Panorama Walk leads to World's End and then the Path crosses desolate (and fairly trackless) moorland to the village of Llandegla. 3 miles more and you are at the foot of the Clwyds.

AREA 10

Clwydian Hills

(A) 5 miles and (B) 7 miles, with extensions of (C) 2½ and (D) 2 miles.

O.S. 1:50,000. 116; O.S. 1:25,000. SJ 16 for main routes, extensions go on to SJ 06, 07, 17.
Grid references are to these maps.

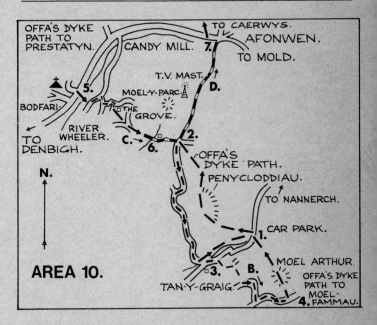

How to get there: By car: Leave Mold on A541 Denbigh road; in 5½ miles go left for Nannerch and immediately left, Llandyrnog turn; in 2½ miles park at the highest point, (1) (139669). For extensions cars may be left at Bodfari or Afonwen on A541.

By public transport: Crossville Mold-Denbigh service serves Afonwen and Bodfari; the Denbigh-Llangwyfan Hospital route (some buses go on to Ruthin) terminates one mile from the suggested car park but only ½ mile from the nearest point on the route, (3) (131664). No Sunday buses.

Refreshments: Inns and village shops at Bodfari, Afonwen and Llandyrnog (2½ miles west of car park).

The 14 miles between the foot of the Clwyds and Bodfari are as exhilarating as any on the whole route with ridge walks, peaks, hill-forts and views as far as Snowdonia. Mold, Ruthin and Denbigh are within reach and it is in the northern part of this setting that the tenth group of walks are located.

From the car park referred to, (1) (139669), take wicket gate on right into Llangwyfan/Clwyd Forest. Offa's Dyke Path is the highest on the right (not a forest ride) and follows the edge of the woods below the fence along the crest of the ridge. Cross stile and up sunken track to the ramparts of the southern corner of the hillfort of Penycloddiau, ²/₃ mile from the start of the walk.

The circuit of the ramparts is a full mile, in places they are tripled and the interior covers 50 acres. The views in all directions are extensive. Offa's Dyke Path goes up the western ramparts (the rest of the circuit is **not** included in the route mileage!).

Grass paths through heather slowly drop in under a mile to a pass at over 1,000 feet, (2) (121690). Ahead is the northernmost of the Clywdian range, Moel-y-Parc with its television mast. Here four ancient roadways cross, Offa's Dyke Path descending to Bodfari being the one going left at 90° (this route is described later). This walk, however, takes the route **very** sharp left. This contours, very slightly dropping for two miles to reach the Nannerch-Llandrynog road again, (3) (131664) just above Tan-y-Graig (the nearest point to the Llangwyfan Hospital bus route).

Two routes are possible from here; the shorter (A) to complete the 5 mile round, is to re-enter the forest immediately on the left and take the Forestry track directly uphill with stream below on your right. This winds and in ²/₃ mile reaches the car park by the road, (1).

For the longer route (B) cross stream by road. After 100 yards, through gate on right and head diagonally left uphill to edge of field. Follow edge, through gate on left and left uphill to two pine trees, leaving farm on right. Cross farm drive and take green lane opposite uphill. When this reaches col, contour to left, aiming at prominent hawthorn on track through bracken. Eventually join broad track, coming from right, in patch of trees. Forward through gate and contour on track right round head of valley, on right, to reach tarred road. Then left and upwards to top of the pass between Moel Llys-y-Coed and Moel Arthur, (4), (146657).

The route now rejoins the Offa's Dyke Path to go northwards along the crest of the Clwyds. First the steep climb to the top of the tiny but well-defined hill-fort on Moel Arthur. The route goes straight up to the top but it can be made much easier by continuing along the road for 200 yards to a path which climbs diagonally. From this you can turn back to the summit which with its triple lines of defences and steep gradients on all but the northern side, is indeed impressive. Clwyd County Council have bought the hill and designated it as a country park. The route from the summit lies north-westwards gradually dropping over a well-marked path to reach the car park at (1) in over ½ mile. (Halfway, in field corner, with fences on left and ahead, stile in corner is well concealed).

The two extensions are the Offa's Dyke Path from Bodfari to the pass at point (2) of 2½ miles (C), and the route from that point northwards to the A541 at Afonwen—2 miles (D). If travelling by bus outward from Bodfari to (2) and return to Afonwen is recommended, inserting of course the round described above starting and finishing at point (2). If a car is used the National Footpath to and from Bodfari, leaving the vehicle at this point, is pleasant. We have as yet not found a satisfactory route from Afonwen to Bodfari (see, however, under Afonwen extension below) and would be pleased to hear of one to complete this northern circuit.

Route C

From the Downing Arms at Bodfari, (5) (098702), turn right on main road for 50 yards, left through gate immediately followed by stile. Cross old railway track and river Wheeler to small road. Left up lane for 200 yards, then right and immediately left to road rising towards TV mast on skyline. Take first right turn at pillar box (The Grove) and immediately past house on left cross stile (with acorn mark and concrete Offa's Dyke marker).

Cross field to next stile with Grove Farm on right, cross stile and contour forward with wire fence on left, cross next stile and climb to the left to old stile. Continue climbing diagonally to acorn-marked stile, cross this and climb further diagonally right to stile by gate at head of sunken green lane. After 200 yards join larger track and continue climbing, then contouring along hillside on unfenced track which eventually drops to cross stream just below farm (Tynewydd), (114692), and rises again to iron gate. This part of the track is roughly metalled.

Beyond this the track has hedge on left, then on both sides and soon reaches a stile above ruined farm buildings. From here it is an easy climb to the pass to join the circular walk, (2) (121690).

The Afonwen route (D) is left from this point (straight forward from the Offa's Dyke Path coming northwards to the pass) along broad unmetalled track leading towards the TV mast. In ½ mile it acquires a metal surface and descends steeply to reach the A541, (7) (131716).

From here the little 'planned town' at Caerwys, an Edward I creation with a late Decorated church, may be reached in a mile. Turn left on the A541 and in ¼ mile take the footpath right by Pwllgwyn Hotel to Caerwys. It is possible to go by small roads westwards from here for 3 miles to join Offa's Dyke Path on the north side of Cefn Du (094732) and then southwards for 2½ miles to Bodfari. The quickest route from Afonwen to Bodfari is 1½ miles west on A541 then take minor road left at Candy Mill; in 2 miles the Long Distance path is reached just east of Bodfari.

Going north from Bodfari the Path crosses lower hills until it emerges on a cliff edge two miles south-west of Prestatyn with sands and contemporary holiday appurtenances between you and the sea. On to the southern end of Prestatyn, down Fford-Las—the main street—past station, shops and candy floss stalls to the sea front. You have arrived at the end of Offa's Dyke Path!

Notes

Public Transport

Rail is relevant only to Areas 1 (Tintern from Chepstow), 6 (Knighton), and 8 (Oswestry via Gobowen). Please consult current British Rail timetables.

Buses are generally infrequent even where services do exist and are prone to withdrawal or alteration to timings. Most companies will supply timetables in return for s.a.e. though sometimes a small charge is involved. Timetables are seldom displayed in the towns and villages concerned. Names and addresses of companies mentioned in the text are:

Red & White, The Bulwark, Chepstow, Gwent.
Yeoman Motors Ltd., Canon Pyon, Hereford.
D. J. Staples, Lugg Valley Motors, Leominster.
Teme Valley Motors, Leintwardine, Salop.
Owens Motors, Knighton, Powys.
Valley Motor Services, Bishops Castle, Salop.
Bryn Melyn Motors, Llangollen, Clwyd.
Crosville, Crane Wharf, Chester.

Maps

These are diagrammatic and not to scale. Used with the text and in particular correlating the point indications—(1), (2), (3), etc.—they should enable walkers to find their route. Though expensive to purchase use of Ordnance Survey maps to supplement the sketch maps can be recommended and reference is made on each walk to the appropriate ones.

Bibliography

The following books provide further information about the Long Distance Footpath:

'Through Welsh Border Country' by Mark Richards (Thornhill Press).

'The O.D.A. Book of Offa's Dyke Path' by Frank Noble (Offa's Dyke Services)

'Offa's Dyke Path by John B. Jones (HMSO).

'A Guide to Offa's Dyke Path' by Christopher J. Wright (Constable).

'The Offa's Dyke Path' by Arthur Roberts (Ramblers' Association booklet).

The historical feature can be studied in great depth in Sir Cyril Fox's 'Offa's Dyke' (Oxford University Press for British Academy).

For background on the Welsh Marches, Maxwell Fraser's 'Welsh Border Country' (Batsford) is invaluable.

The Offa's Dyke Association publishes other guide material, strip maps, accommodation lists, badges, etc.

Details of these and of membership are available (s.a.e. please) from O.D.A., West Street, Knighton, Powys.

A WALKER'S GUIDE TO WELSH PLACE NAMES

The Welsh language looks, to the English eye, like a collection of typographical errors and spelling howlers, all of which are quite unpronounceable. Less intrepid visitors give up what appears to be the unequal struggle of trying to pronounce place names correctly or discover their meanings. Thus they lose much of the charm of Wales. The names of villages, mountains and farms are the spice which gives any country its special flavour.

How to pronounce it

The anarchic, unpronounceable appearance of the Welsh language is caused by the fact that a small but crucial number of Welsh letters represent different sounds from those sounds which they represent in English spelling. Take the letter W for example. In Welsh, W is almost always like the double OO in the English word 'moon'. The word *cwm* (a valley) is pronounced COOM. The west country word COOMBE is Welsh in origin and means exactly the same thing. Another problem is the letter F, which in Welsh is always pronounced as a V, as in the word *afon* (a river), which a Welshman pronounces as if it were spelt AVON. In fact, the River Avon in England gets its name directly from Welsh. If you want to write the sound of English F you must write FF in Welsh. A Welshman named Fred, for example, would spell his name FFred.

The letter Y is often pronounced like I in English words such as kit, it, bit etc. So the apparently unpronounceable word *twyn* (a small hill or burial mound) is pronounced TOO-IN. Otherwise, Y is pronounced rather like UH in English: *Twyn-y-gaer* is TOO-IN UH GUYER, fortress hill. In Welsh, the word *Y* means 'the'.

The double LL in Welsh place names fills many with alarm. But it really presents no problems. Properly speaking the double LL is pronounced by placing your tongue behind your front teeth and blowing slightly, making a hissing noise. But it is quite sufficient to pronounce it like the ordinary letter L in English (large numbers of Welsh people do).

A few other things to note: DD in Welsh is pronounced like TH in English. 'Though' in Welsh would be written *'ddo'*. The letter U is often pronounced as 'ee' in the English word bee. *Un* (one) is spoken as 'een'. Combinations of letter such as AE and AU are pronounced just like 'aye' in English; *Maes,* (a field) is pronounced the same as the English word 'mice'.

What does it mean?

Welsh place names are usually descriptions, some of them quite poetic. But the emphasis is on description. Many places begin with the word *aber*, meaning the mouth of a river. Aberyswyth, the mouth of the Ystwyth River; Abertawe (the Welsh name for Swansea), the mouth of the Tawe River. Another class of place names begins with the word *Llan,* a church or parish. Llanfair, the church of (St.) Mary; Llanfihangel, the church of (St.) Michael.

Plurals in Welsh are usually formed by adding the letter AU to the end of a word. An example is *dol* (a meadow); *dolau* (meadows).

A small Welsh-English pocket dictionary would be a useful companion in any walker's rucksack. But for the impecunious here is a small glossary of common words and their meanings:

Glossary

Bach, fach, small	*Dyffryn,* Valley
Bryn, Hill	*Llyn,* Lake
Bwlch, Pass	*Llys,* Hall or Palace
Caer, Gaer, Fort	*Maen,* Stone
Cefn, Ridge	*Mawr, Fawr,* Big
Clawdd, Dyke	*Melin,* Mill
Coed, Wood	*Nant,* Stream
Du, Black	*Pont,* Bridge
Dwr, Water	*Ty,* House

Country Code

Take care to avoid damaging farm property by remembering to: Guard against all risks of fire. Fasten all gates. Keep dogs under proper control. Keep to the paths across farmland. Avoid damaging fences. Hedges and walks. Leave no litter. Safeguard water supplies. Protect wild life. Wild plants and trees. Go carefully on country roads. Respect the life of the countryside.